I0866877

101 THINGS® TO DO WITH

CHOCOLATE

101 THINGS® TO DO WITH
CHOCOLATE

STEPHANIE ASHCRAFT

Gibbs Smith

Second Edition
29 28 27 26 25 5 4 3 2 1

First Gibbs Smith edition published in 2008
Second Gibbs Smith edition published August 2025

Published by
Gibbs Smith
570 N. Sportsplex Drive
Kaysville, Utah 84037
1.800.835.4993 orders
www.gibbs-smith.com

Designed by Ryan Thomann and Renee Bond
Printed and bound in China

The Library of Congress has cataloged the first edition as follows:
101 things to do with chocolate / Stephanie Ashcraft.
p. cm.
ISBN-13: 978-1-4236-0180-7
1. Cookery (Chocolate) 2. Desserts. I. Title. II. Title: One hundred and one things to do with chocolate.
TX767.C5A74 2007
641.6'374—dc22
2007029135

ISBN: 978-1-4236-6879-4
eISBN: 978-1-4236-1228-5

This product is made of FSC®-certified and other controlled material.

MIX
Paper | Supporting responsible forestry
FSC® C144853
FSC
www.fsc.org

To my husband and children, thank you for
all your support throughout the years.

To all my family in Indiana and Illinois, thank you for
always loving and encouraging me in all that I do.

To all my Ashcraft family, thank you for allowing
me to be your "favorite" aunt and sister-in-law.
You're all my favorites, too.

To my parents, thank you for teaching me correct
principles and giving me the room and direction to fly.

I love you all.

CONTENTS

#55–64 Ice Cream Cakes & Sandwiches

#65–74 Cheesecakes, Dessert Pizzas & Pies

#75–89 Family Favorites

#90–101 Trifles & Entertaining Ideas

Helpful Hints

- Remember that chocolate can be easily scorched or ruined. Whether melting chocolate in a heavy pan, double boiler, slow cooker, or microwave, gently heat chocolate, stirring frequently until melted. Never leave melting chocolate unattended; it will burn if not watched carefully. Avoid getting any water in the chocolate, as water will create clumps. If this happens, add 1 teaspoon to 1 tablespoon shortening or butter to the chocolate and stir until smooth.
- Melting chocolate can be done in the microwave. Make sure the microwave-safe dish you are using is completely dry. Microwave 1 cup chocolate chips on high for 45 seconds. Chocolate should be half melted. If not, microwave an additional 30 seconds. Remove and stir until chocolate lumps melt completely.
- Dipping chocolate is one of my family's favorite things to do. When I am ready to dip, I melt my chocolate in the slow cooker. The chocolate can be left on low heat, stirring occasionally to break up any chocolate lumps. You can take your time dipping with this method. With other methods, you have to hurry to use the chocolate before it hardens again.
- It can be easy to make chocolate candy. Many craft stores sell candy molds and chocolate candy melts. Heat the candy melts in a small slow cooker on high heat. Once melted, turn heat to low. Spoon chocolate into ungreased molds. Tap filled molds on the table to remove any air bubbles. Place molds in the freezer 15 minutes or

until chocolate is hard. If making suckers, be sure to place the sucker stick in the chocolate and then give it a full twist to assure it will stay in the sucker.

- Store chocolate in a covered or an airtight container in a cool, dry place. If storing in the refrigerator or freezer, allow chocolate to come to room temperature before adding it to a recipe.
- Chocolate will sometimes start to turn gray on the outside, especially when it becomes too warm. The chocolate is still good and will return to its natural color once melted.
- Milk chocolate chips can be used in place of semisweet chips in any recipe. Milk chocolate chips are sweeter and creamier than semisweet chips, but semisweet chocolate adds a rich, denser chocolate taste to recipes.
- My favorite chocolate cake mix is Betty Crocker Triple Chocolate Fudge. It can be used in any recipe calling for a chocolate cake mix.
- Always grease and flour the cake pan or spray it with oil—even when the recipe doesn't call for it.
- Bake cakes on the middle oven rack, never on the top or bottom racks.
- For best results, use glass or stoneware baking dishes.
- For chewier cookies and bars, take them out of the oven just as they begin to turn golden brown around the edges and let them cool on or in the pan.

#1–9

CANDIES

#1

Easy Holiday Mint Truffles

MAKES 20 TRUFFLES

2/3 cup	**whipping cream**
1 bag (11.5 ounces)	**semisweet chocolate chips**
1 to 1 1/2 teaspoons	**mint extract**
	sweetened coconut flakes, chopped chocolate chips, chopped mint chips or Andes Mints, or chopped candy canes for topping

In a saucepan, heat whipping cream until it starts to boil. Remove from heat; immediately stir in chocolate chips and mint extract. Stir until chips melt completely. Pour into a medium bowl. Cover with plastic wrap and refrigerate 2–3 hours, or until firm.

Line a baking sheet with wax paper. Drop heaping teaspoons of chocolate mixture onto wax paper. Place baking sheet in freezer and freeze chocolates 40–50 minutes. Place desired toppings in separate bowls. Shape frozen truffles into 1-inch balls and then roll in toppings. Cover and refrigerate 2 hours. Store truffles in an airtight container in the refrigerator.

#2

Peanut Butter Chocolate Candy

MAKES 30–35 CANDIES

1 cup	**crunchy or creamy peanut butter**
½ cup	**butter or margarine, melted**
3½ cups	**powdered sugar**
1 bag (11.5 ounces)	**chocolate chips**

In a large bowl, combine peanut butter and butter. Stir in powdered sugar. Knead with hands until powdered sugar is worked completely into peanut butter mixture. Refrigerate if not being used immediately.

Form peanut butter dough into small balls about 1 inch in diameter and place on wax paper. Melt chocolate chips in a microwave-safe dish, stirring every 30 seconds, until smooth. Roll balls in chocolate and place back onto wax paper. Refrigerate at least 1 hour, or until chocolate hardens.

#3

Decadent Chocolate Truffles

MAKES 35 TRUFFLES

2 cups	**semisweet chocolate chips**
1 cup	**milk chocolate chips**
1 can (14 ounces)	**sweetened condensed milk**
1 tablespoon	**vanilla**
	finely chopped nuts, sweetened coconut flakes, cake decorating sprinkles, powdered sugar, or cocoa powder for topping

In a heavy 2-quart pan, melt together chocolate chips and condensed milk; stir in vanilla. Refrigerate 2 or more hours in the pan until firm.

Place desired toppings in separate bowls. Shape chocolate into small balls about 1 inch in diameter and then roll in toppings. Store in the refrigerator until ready to serve.

#4

Cream Cheese Truffles

MAKES 40 TRUFFLES

1 package (8 ounces)	**cream cheese, softened**
3 cups	**powdered sugar, sifted**
2 cups	**milk chocolate chips**
1 cup	**semisweet chocolate chips**
1 tablespoon	**vanilla**
	finely chopped nuts, sweetened coconut flakes, cake decorating sprinkles, powdered sugar, or cocoa powder for topping

In a bowl, combine cream cheese and powdered sugar with a hand mixer until smooth. Melt chocolate chips together and then stir melted chocolate and vanilla into powdered sugar mixture until it turns an even brown color. Refrigerate 2 hours.

Place desired toppings in separate bowls. Shape chocolate into small balls about 1 inch in diameter and then roll in toppings.

Variation: Use 1 cup peanut butter chips in place of semisweet chocolate chips.

#5

Fun-Topped Fudge

MAKES 16–20 SERVINGS

4 1/2 cups	**sugar**
1 can (12 ounces)	**evaporated milk**
1/2 cup	**butter or margarine, melted**
1 bag (11.5 ounces)	**semisweet chocolate chips**
1 jar (7 ounces)	**marshmallow creme**
3/4 cup	**chopped nuts, crushed Butterfinger, crushed candy cane, mint baking chips, or mini M&M's for topping**

In a nonstick pan, bring sugar, milk, and butter to a boil. Boil 6–8 minutes, stirring constantly. Turn off heat and stir in chocolate chips and marshmallow creme. Spread fudge evenly into a greased 8 x 8-inch or 9 x 9-inch pan. Chill at least 1 hour before sprinkling toppings over top. Lightly press topping into fudge; refrigerate overnight.

#6

Brown Family Orange Sticks

MAKES 35–40 CHOCOLATE ORANGE STICKS

2 cups	**water**
2 cups	**sugar**
2	**oranges**
2 bars (5 ounces each)	**dark chocolate**

In a 3-quart saucepan, boil together water and sugar over medium heat. While waiting for mixture to boil, use a knife or orange peeler to remove the peel in four even sections from each orange; thick peel works the best. Save oranges for another use. Cut each section into five long slices about 1/4-inch thick. Orange peel slices will be about the same size as thin french fries.

Once mixture begins to boil, add orange peel slices and lightly boil for 10 minutes, or until the orange peels are saturated with the sugar. Orange peels will become translucent. Strain the peels and set aside.

Break bars of chocolate into small pieces and place in a small slow cooker. Stir chocolate over high heat until it melts; turn heat to low. Using a fork or toothpick, dip each orange peel slice into the melted chocolate until coated completely. Lay chocolate orange sticks on wax paper placed on a baking sheet. Place pan in freezer for 15 minutes to harden chocolate. Store in the refrigerator.

#7

Chocolate-Coated Cookie Balls

MAKES 35–40 CANDIES

1 bag (1 pound)	**chocolate sandwich cookies, chopped**
1 package (8 ounces)	**cream cheese, softened**
20 ounces	**chocolate almond bark, melted**

In a large bowl, combine chopped cookies and cream cheese to form dough. Roll into small balls about 1 to 1½ inches in diameter. Using a fork, dip balls into melted chocolate. Set balls on wax paper and chill 1 hour, or until set.

Variations: Use chocolate mint sandwich cookies, chocolate peanut butter filled sandwich cookies, or any other variation of sandwich cookies.

#8

Chocolate Butter Nut Crunch

MAKES 8–10 SERVINGS

1 cup sugar
1/4 cup water
1/2 cup butter or margarine
1/2 teaspoon salt
1 1/2 cups chocolate chips, divided
1/2 cup finely chopped nuts, divided

In a 2-quart nonstick pan, combine sugar, water, butter, and salt. Boil until mixture reaches 290 degrees on a candy thermometer. Pour onto a greased baking sheet and let cool.

In the microwave, melt half the chocolate chips 45–60 seconds. Stir and spread chocolate over hardened candy. Sprinkle half the nuts over top. Place baking sheet in freezer for 20 minutes and allow chocolate to harden; flip candy. Melt remaining chocolate chips and spread over uncovered side of candy. Sprinkle remaining nuts over top. Freeze an additional 20 minutes. Once chocolate hardens, break candy into pieces.

#9

Rocky Road Drops

MAKES 36–45 DROPS

2 cups	**milk chocolate chips**
1 can (14 ounces)	**sweetened condensed milk**
3½ cups	**miniature marshmallows**
2½ cups	**salted dry roasted peanuts**

In a heavy saucepan, melt chocolate with condensed milk over low heat. Once chocolate is completely melted and smooth, remove from heat.

In a large bowl, combine marshmallows and nuts. Stir in chocolate mixture. Drop by spoonfuls onto wax paper and then refrigerate 2 hours, or until set.

#10–23

COOKIES

#10

Vanilla Chocolate Chip Cookies

MAKES 36 COOKIES

1 cup	**butter or margarine, softened**
3/4 cup	**brown sugar**
1/4 cup	**sugar**
1 small box	**vanilla instant pudding mix**
2	**eggs**
1 teaspoon	**vanilla**
2 1/4 cups	**flour**
1 teaspoon	**baking soda**
1/4 teaspoon	**salt**
3/4 cup	**semisweet chocolate chips**
1 1/4 cups	**milk chocolate chips**

Preheat oven to 350 degrees.

In a large bowl, combine butter, brown sugar, and sugar. Stir in pudding mix, eggs, and vanilla.

In a separate bowl, combine flour, baking soda, and salt. Slowly stir flour mixture into pudding mixture. Stir in chocolate chips. Drop heaping teaspoons of dough onto a lightly greased baking sheet. Bake 10–12 minutes, or until lightly golden around the edges.

#11

Coconut Cream Chocolate Chip Cookies

MAKES 36 COOKIES

2 1/4 cups	**flour**
1 teaspoon	**baking soda**
1 cup	**butter or margarine, softened**
1/4 cup	**sugar**
3/4 cup	**brown sugar**
1 teaspoon	**vanilla**
1 small box	**coconut cream instant pudding mix**
2	**eggs**
1 1/2 cups	**semisweet chocolate chips**
1 cup	**sweetened coconut flakes**

Preheat oven to 375 degrees.

In a medium bowl, combine flour and baking soda.

In a large bowl, combine butter, sugar, brown sugar, and vanilla; mix until smooth. Beat in pudding mix and eggs. Slowly stir in flour mixture followed by chocolate chips and coconut. Drop heaping teaspoons of dough onto a lightly greased baking sheet. Bake 9–10 minutes, or until lightly golden around the edges.

#12

Chocolate Butter Pecan Cookies

MAKES 36 COOKIES

1 box	**chocolate cake mix**
2	**eggs**
½ cup	**butter or margarine, melted**
1 container (15 ounces)	**coconut pecan frosting**

Preheat oven to 350 degrees.

In a bowl, mix cake mix, eggs, butter, and frosting together until smooth. Refrigerate dough 1–2 hours. Drop heaping teaspoons of dough onto a lightly greased baking sheet. Bake 10–12 minutes. Remove from pan and place cookies on a nonstick cooling rack.

#13

Nutty Chocolate Chip Cereal Cookies

MAKES 40–45 COOKIES

2/3 cup butter-flavored shortening or butter
1/2 cup brown sugar, firmly packed
2 eggs
1 box chocolate cake mix
1 cup crispy rice cereal
1 cup white, semisweet, or milk chocolate chips
1/2 cup chopped nuts

Preheat oven to 350 degrees.

In a bowl, blend shortening or butter and brown sugar together. Beat eggs in one at a time and then stir in cake mix. With a spoon, stir in cereal, chocolate chips, and nuts. Drop heaping teaspoons of dough onto a lightly greased baking sheet. Bake 9–12 minutes, or until tops look cracked. Do not overbake. Cool 2–3 minutes on baking sheet and then remove cookies and place on a nonstick cooling rack to cool.

#14

Oatmeal Chocolate Chip Cookies

MAKES 36–42 COOKIES

1 cup	**shortening or butter**
3/4 cup	**brown sugar**
3/4 cup	**sugar**
1 teaspoon	**vanilla**
2	**eggs**
1 1/2 cups	**flour**
1 teaspoon	**baking soda**
1 teaspoon	**salt**
1 1/2 cups	**rolled oats**
1 1/2 cups	**semisweet chocolate chips**

Preheat oven to 350 degrees.

In a large bowl, combine shortening or butter, sugars, and vanilla. Beat in eggs until thoroughly mixed.

In a separate bowl, combine flour, baking soda, salt, and oats. Stir into creamy mixture and then add chocolate chips. Drop teaspoons of dough onto a lightly greased baking sheet. Bake 10–12 minutes, or until lightly golden around the edges.

#15

Peanut Butter Chocolate Chip Cookies

MAKES 30–36 COOKIES

1 box	**devil's food cake mix**
2	**eggs**
½ cup	**butter or margarine, softened**
½ cup	**chunky peanut butter**
1 cup	**chocolate chips**

Preheat oven to 350 degrees.

In a bowl, mix together cake mix, eggs, and butter until dough forms. Stir in peanut butter and chocolate chips. Drop teaspoons of dough onto a lightly greased baking sheet. Bake 10–11 minutes. Remove from pan and cool.

Variation: To make bars, spread dough evenly into a lightly greased 9 x 13-inch pan. Bake 18–20 minutes.

#16

No-Bake Chocolate Drops

MAKES 20 COOKIES

1 cup	**chocolate chips**
⅓ cup	**butter or margarine**
18 large	**marshmallows**
½ teaspoon	**vanilla**
1 cup	**sweetened coconut flakes**
2 cups	**rolled oats**

In a 3-quart heavy pan, combine chocolate chips, butter, and marshmallows. Stir constantly over medium heat until marshmallows and chocolate are melted; remove pan from heat. Stir in vanilla and then fold in coconut and rolled oats. Drop spoonfuls of mixture onto wax paper and cool before serving.

#17

Pumpkin Chocolate Chip Cookies

MAKES 30–36 COOKIES

1 box	**yellow or spice cake mix**
1 can (15 ounces)	**solid pack pumpkin**
1 cup	**semisweet or milk chocolate chips**

Preheat oven to 350 degrees.

In a large bowl, mix together cake mix and pumpkin until well blended. Stir in chocolate chips. Drop rounded spoonfuls of dough onto a lightly greased baking sheet. Bake 8–10 minutes. Allow cookies to cool on baking sheet 5 minutes before transferring to a wire rack to cool completely.

#18

Macadamia Nut Chocolate Cookies

MAKES 36–40 COOKIES

1 box	**chocolate cake mix**
2	**eggs**
½ cup	**butter or margarine, softened**
1 cup	**white chocolate chunks or chips**
½ cup	**chopped macadamia nuts**

Preheat oven to 350 degrees.

In a bowl, mix together cake mix, eggs, and butter. Mixture should be stiff and all the cake mix should be mixed into the dough. Stir in white chocolate and nuts. Use cookie scoop to drop dough onto an ungreased baking sheet. Bake 10–11 minutes. Remove from pan and place on nonstick cooling rack to cool.

Variation: 1 cup semisweet or milk chocolate chips or chunks can be substituted in place of white chocolate.

#19

Chocolate Chunk Cookies

MAKES 36–40 COOKIES

1 box	**chocolate cake mix**
2	**eggs**
1/2 cup	**butter or margarine, softened**
1 cup	**rolled oats**
1/2 cup	**chopped pecans or walnuts**
3/4 cup	**sweetened coconut flakes**
3 (1.55 ounces each)	**milk chocolate candy bars, cut into 1/4- to 1/2-inch chunks**

Preheat oven to 350 degrees.

In a bowl, mix together cake mix, eggs, and butter. Mixture should be stiff and all the cake mix should be mixed into the dough. Stir in oats, pecans, coconut, and chocolate chunks. Use cookie scoop to drop dough onto a baking sheet. Bake 10–12 minutes. Remove from pan and place on nonstick cooling rack to cool.

Variation: 1 cup semisweet or white chocolate chips can be substituted in place of the chocolate chunks.

#20

Chocolate Chip Cookies

MAKES 52–60 COOKIES

1 cup	**brown sugar**
½ cup	**sugar**
1 cup	**shortening or butter, softened**
2	**eggs**
1 teaspoon	**vanilla**
2½ cups	**flour**
1 teaspoon	**baking soda**
¾ teaspoon	**salt**
1 package (11.5 ounces)	**chocolate chips**

Preheat oven to 350 degrees.

In a large bowl, cream together sugars with shortening or butter. Stir in eggs, one at a time; add vanilla.

In a separate bowl, combine flour, baking soda, and salt. Slowly stir flour mixture into sugar mixture. Stir in chocolate chips. Drop teaspoons of dough onto a baking sheet. Bake 10 minutes, or until lightly golden around the edges.

Variation: My great-grandmother would sometimes stir in 1½ cups crispy rice cereal to this family-favorite cookie dough.

#21

Chocolate Chip Sandwich Cookies

MAKES 15–18 SANDWICH COOKIES

Filling:

1½ cups	**milk**
½ cup	**creamy peanut butter**
1 small box	**chocolate instant pudding mix**

Cookies:

1 box	**white cake mix**
2	**eggs**
⅓ cup	**canola oil**
1 cup	**chocolate chips**

For the filling, in a 2-quart bowl, whisk together milk and peanut butter. Whisk in chocolate pudding mix and then refrigerate until ready to use.

For the cookies, preheat oven to 350 degrees.

In a 2-quart bowl, combine cake mix, eggs, and oil until cookie dough forms. Stir in chocolate chips. Drop teaspoons of dough onto a baking sheet. Bake 8–11 minutes, or until lightly golden around the edges. Do not overcook. Allow cookies to cool. Place a scoop of pudding mixture between two cookies. Store in refrigerator.

Variation: For peanut butter cookies, stir in ½ cup peanut butter into cookie dough before baking.

#22

Peanut Butter Candy Cookies

MAKES 36 COOKIES

1 box	**chocolate cake mix**
2	**eggs**
1/2 cup	**butter or margarine, softened**
1/2 cup	**crunchy peanut butter**
1 to 1 1/2 cups	**plain M&M's**

Preheat oven to 350 degrees.

In a large bowl, mix together cake mix, eggs, butter, and peanut butter until cake mix is thoroughly moistened. Stir M&M's into dough. Use a cookie scoop to drop dough onto a baking sheet. Bake 9–12 minutes. Allow cookies to set up on hot baking sheet 2–3 minutes. Remove from pan and place on nonstick cooling rack to cool.

#23

Rolo Surprise Cookies

MAKES 36 COOKIES

1 box white or chocolate cake mix
2 eggs
½ cup butter or margarine, softened
36 individual Rolo candies, unwrapped

Heat oven to 350 degrees.

In a bowl, mix together cake mix, eggs, and butter until cake mix is thoroughly moistened. Place a Rolo candy in the center of a teaspoon of dough. Roll dough around candy, making sure the candy is completely covered with dough. Place onto a baking sheet. Bake 10 minutes. Allow to cool before serving.

#24–31

BROWNIES

#24

Pink Peppermint Frosted Brownies

MAKES 24 BROWNIES

1 box (9 x 13-inch family size)	**brownie mix**
	ingredients listed on back of box
	red food coloring
1 container (16 ounces)	**vanilla frosting**
1 bag (10 ounces)	**Andes Peppermint Crunch Baking Chips**
3 tablespoons	**butter or margarine**
3 (1 ounce each)	**unsweetened or semisweet chocolate squares**

Preheat oven to 350 degrees.

Prepare and bake brownies according to package directions in a greased 9 x 13-inch pan; cool. Stir drops of red food coloring into vanilla frosting until it reaches desired shade of pink. Frost brownies with pink frosting. Sprinkle peppermint chips over top.

In a small saucepan, melt butter and chocolate squares. Drizzle over top of brownies. Cool completely before cutting into squares.

#25

Rocky Road Brownies

MAKES 24 BROWNIES

1 box (9 x 13-inch family size) brownie mix
ingredients listed on back of box
1 cup salted peanuts
2 cups miniature marshmallows
1 cup chocolate chips

Preheat oven to 350 degrees.

Make batter according to package directions. Pour batter into a greased 9 x 13-inch pan. Bake 23–25 minutes. Remove brownies from oven. Sprinkle peanuts, marshmallows, and chocolate chips evenly over top. Bake an additional 3–5 minutes, or until marshmallows puff up.

#26

Doctored-Up Brownies

MAKES 24 BROWNIES

1 box (9 x 13-inch family size)	**brownie mix**
	ingredients listed on back of box
¾ cup	**M&M's, Reese's Pieces, mint chocolate pieces, peanut butter chips, butterscotch chips, chocolate chips, white chocolate chips, or nuts**
1 container (16 ounces)	**chocolate frosting**

Preheat oven to 350 degrees.

Make batter according to package directions. Stir in M&M's (or other candy item). Pour batter into a greased 9 x 13-inch pan. Bake 25 minutes, or until done. Allow brownies to cool. Spread frosting evenly over brownies. Sprinkle any extra candies over top.

Variation: Use a 9 x 9-inch size brownie mix with ½ cup candy, nuts, or baking chips.

#27

Chocolate Mint Layer Brownies

MAKES 24 BROWNIES

1 box (9 x 13-inch family size) **brownie mix**
ingredients listed on back of box

Mint Layer:

2 cups **powdered sugar**
½ cup **butter or margarine, softened**
1½ teaspoons **mint extract**
3 or 4 drops **green food coloring**

Chocolate Layer:

2 tablespoons **butter or margarine**
1 cup **semisweet or mint chocolate chips**
1½ tablespoons **milk**

Preheat oven to 350 degrees.

Prepare and bake brownies according to package directions in a 9 x 13-inch pan. Allow brownies to cool completely.

For the mint layer, combine powdered sugar, butter, mint extract, and food coloring. Spread over cooled brownies.

For the chocolate layer, melt together butter, chocolate chips, and milk in a small saucepan. Spread over mint layer and allow to cool. Store leftovers in the refrigerator.

#28

Cookie Dough Brownies

MAKES 24 BROWNIES

Bottom Layer:

1 box (9 x 13-inch family size) brownie mix
ingredients listed on back of box
½ cup semisweet chocolate chips

Filling:

½ cup butter or margarine, softened
½ cup brown sugar
¼ cup sugar
2 tablespoons milk
1 teaspoon vanilla
1 cup flour

Topping:

1 tablespoon butter or margarine
1 cup semisweet chocolate chips
nuts of choice (optional)

Preheat oven to 350 degrees.

For the bottom layer, make batter according to package directions. Stir in chocolate chips. Pour batter into a greased 9 x 13-inch pan. Bake 25 minutes, or until done. Allow brownies to cool completely.

For the filling, mix butter and sugars together in a bowl. Stir in milk and vanilla; mix in flour. Spread filling evenly over cooled brownies.

For the topping, in a small saucepan, melt together butter and chocolate chips. Spread melted chocolate over filling. Nuts can be sprinkled on top, if desired. Cut into bars and refrigerate at least 2 hours; store leftovers in the refrigerator.

#29

Easy Brownies from Scratch

MAKES 10–12 BROWNIES

3/4 cup	**butter or margarine, melted**
1 1/4 cups	**sugar**
1 1/2 teaspoons	**vanilla**
2	**eggs**
3/4 cup	**flour**
1/2 cup	**baking cocoa**
1/4 teaspoon	**salt**
3/4 cup	**chocolate chips**

Preheat oven to 350 degrees.

In a large bowl, combine butter, sugar, and vanilla; beat in eggs.

In a separate bowl, combine flour, cocoa, and salt. Slowly stir flour mixture into cream mixture. Pour batter into a greased 8 x 8-inch pan. Sprinkle chocolate chips over top and then bake 30–35 minutes; allow brownies to cool.

Variations: Use 3/4 cup peanut butter chips in place of chocolate chips. Chopped Andes Mints or butterscotch chips can also be used in place of chocolate chips.

#30

Caramel Cashew Brownies

MAKES 24 BROWNIES

1 box (9 x 13-inch family size) brownie mix
ingredients listed on back of box
1 cup chopped cashews
1 cup semisweet or milk chocolate chips
25 caramels, unwrapped
1/8 cup milk

Preheat oven to 350 degrees.

Make batter according to package directions. Stir in cashews and chocolate chips. Pour batter into a greased 9 x 13-inch pan. Bake 25 minutes, or until done; allow bars to cool 20–30 minutes.

In a saucepan, thoroughly melt caramels and milk together, stirring constantly. Pour caramel topping evenly over brownies. Cool completely and cut into bars.

#31

Peanut Butter Cup Brownies

MAKES 24 BROWNIES

20	**miniature peanut butter cups**
1 box (9 x 13-inch family size)	**brownie mix**
2	**eggs**
½ cup	**vegetable oil**
¼ cup	**water**

Preheat oven to 350 degrees.

Unwrap and cut peanut butter cups in half.

In a bowl, mix together brownie mix, eggs, oil, and water. Stir in peanut butter cups. Pour batter into a greased 9 x 13-inch pan. Bake 28–30 minutes.

#32-44

BARS

#32

Chocolate Caramel Candy Bars

MAKES 24 BARS

1 box	**chocolate cake mix**
1/2 cup	**butter or margarine, melted**
1/4 cup	**evaporated milk**
1 cup	**chocolate chips**
3/4 cup	**chopped nuts**
1 jar (12 ounces)	**caramel ice cream topping**

Preheat oven to 350 degrees.

In a bowl, mix together cake mix, butter, and milk until dough forms. Press three-fourths of the dough evenly into a greased 9 x 13-inch pan. Spread chocolate chips and nuts evenly over the dough. Pour caramel evenly over top. Break the rest of the dough into small pieces and drop evenly over the caramel. Bake 20–25 minutes. Cool 30 minutes and then cut into bars and refrigerate.

#33

Chocolate Peanut Layer Bars

MAKES 24 BARS

Bottom Layer:

1 box	**chocolate cake mix**
4 tablespoons	**butter or margarine, melted**
2	**eggs**
½ cup	**creamy peanut butter**

Top Layer:

1 can (14 ounces)	**sweetened condensed milk**
1 cup	**chocolate chips**
1 cup	**peanut butter chips**
½ cup	**chopped peanuts**

Preheat oven to 350 degrees.

For the bottom layer, in a bowl, mix together cake mix, butter, eggs, and peanut butter. Press dough evenly into a lightly greased 9 x 13-inch pan.

For the top layer, pour sweetened condensed milk over the dough layer. Sprinkle chocolate chips, peanut butter chips, and peanuts evenly over top. Bake 20–25 minutes. Cool completely and cut into bars.

#34

Peanut Butter Chip Cookie Bars

MAKES 24 BARS

1 box	**chocolate cake mix**
2	**eggs**
1/2 cup	**butter or margarine, melted**
3/4 cup	**chunky peanut butter**
1 cup	**peanut butter chips**

Preheat oven to 350 degrees.

In a bowl, mix together cake mix, eggs, butter, and peanut butter until dough forms. Stir in peanut butter chips. Spread dough evenly into a greased 9 x 13-inch pan. Bake 23–25 minutes. Cut into bars and serve warm or at room temperature.

Variation: For rich chocolate bars, use semisweet chocolate chips in place of peanut butter chips.

#35

Chocolate Fall Harvest Bars

MAKES 24 BARS

1 box	**devil's food cake mix**
2	**eggs**
½ cup	**vegetable oil or butter or margarine, melted**
½ cup	**Skor toffee bits or crushed Butterfinger bars**
½ cup	**chocolate chips**

Preheat oven to 350 degrees.

In a bowl, mix together cake mix, eggs, and oil until dough forms. Stir in candy bits and chocolate chips. Spread dough evenly into a lightly greased 9 x 13-inch pan. Bake 18–20 minutes. Cut into bars and serve warm or at room temperature.

#36

Chocolate Peanut Butter Fantasy Bars

MAKES 24 BARS

1 box	**chocolate cake mix**
½ cup	**butter or margarine, melted**
1	**egg**
1½ cups	**sweetened coconut flakes**
1 can (14 ounces)	**sweetened condensed milk**
2 cups	**semisweet chocolate chips**
½ cup	**creamy peanut butter**

Preheat oven to 350 degrees.

In a bowl, mix together cake mix, butter, and egg until smooth. Press dough evenly into a lightly greased 9 x 13-inch glass pan. Sprinkle coconut over the top. Pour sweetened condensed milk evenly over coconut. Bake 20–25 minutes, or until edges are a light golden brown.

In a saucepan, melt together chocolate chips and peanut butter over low heat. Spread chocolate over hot top layer. Cool 30 minutes. Refrigerate and cut into bars.

#37

Chocolate Layer Bars

MAKES 24 BARS

1 box	**chocolate cake mix**
½ cup	**butter or margarine, melted**
1	**egg**
1 can (14 ounces)	**sweetened condensed milk**
1 cup	**sweetened coconut flakes**
1 cup	**chocolate chips**
1 cup	**butterscotch chips**
1 bag (2 ounces)	**sliced almonds**

Preheat oven to 350 degrees.

In a bowl, mix together cake mix, butter, and egg. Press dough evenly into a lightly greased 9 x 13-inch pan. Pour sweetened condensed milk over the dough layer. Sprinkle coconut, chocolate chips, butterscotch chips, and nuts evenly over top. Bake 25 minutes. Cool completely and cut into bars.

#38

Decadent Semisweet Cookie Bars

MAKES 24 BARS

27	**chocolate sandwich cookies, divided**
4 tablespoons	**butter or margarine, melted**
2 cups	**semisweet chocolate chips, divided**
1 can (14 ounces)	**sweetened condensed milk**
1 teaspoon	**vanilla**

Preheat oven to 325 degrees.

Grind 21 of the cookies in a blender or food processor.

In a bowl, combine cookie crumbs and butter. Press crumb mixture evenly into a lightly greased 9 x 13-inch pan.

In a saucepan, combine 1 cup chocolate chips, sweetened condensed milk, and vanilla over low heat, stirring until chocolate melts. Drizzle chocolate sauce evenly over crust. Sprinkle remaining 1 cup chocolate chips over the top. Crumble remaining 6 cookies over top. Bake 20 minutes. Allow to cool. Refrigerate at least 2 hours and cut into bars.

Variations: Use chocolate mint sandwich cookies, chocolate peanut butter–filled sandwich cookies, or any other variation of sandwich cookies.

#39

Peanut Butter Crunch Bars

MAKES 24 BARS

1 box **chocolate cake mix**
2 **eggs**
½ cup **vegetable oil**
½ cup **creamy or crunchy peanut butter**

Topping:

1 cup **semisweet chocolate chips***
½ cup **creamy peanut butter**
1½ cups **crispy rice cereal**

Preheat oven to 350 degrees.

In a bowl, mix together cake mix, eggs, and oil until dough forms. Stir in peanut butter. Spread dough evenly into a lightly greased 9 x 13-inch pan. Bake 18–20 minutes. Cool 20–25 minutes.

For the topping, melt chocolate chips and peanut butter together in a saucepan over low heat. Remove from heat. Fold cereal into melted chocolate sauce. Spread mixture evenly over bars. Cool completely and cut into bars.

*For a sweeter chocolate taste, use milk chocolate chips instead of semisweet chocolate chips.

#40

Chocolate Cream Cheese Bars

MAKES 12 BARS

1 box	**chocolate cake mix**
3	**eggs**
½ cup	**butter or margarine, softened**
1 cup	**semisweet chocolate chips**
1 package (8 ounces)	**cream cheese, softened**
½ cup	**sugar**

Preheat oven to 350 degrees.

In a bowl, mix together cake mix, 2 eggs, and butter until smooth. Stir in chocolate chips. Press two-thirds of the dough evenly into a lightly greased 8 x 8-inch pan.

In a separate bowl, mix together cream cheese, sugar, and remaining 1 egg until fairly smooth. Spread cream cheese mixture over the dough layer. Lay long, flat sections of remaining dough evenly over the top, trying to cover as much as possible. Bake 35 minutes. Allow to cool completely. Refrigerate at least 2 hours before serving.

#41

Chocolate Chip Pudding Bars

MAKES 24 BARS

1 box **yellow or white cake mix**
2 **eggs**
1/3 cup **vegetable oil**
1 cup **chocolate chips**

Topping:

1 small box **chocolate instant pudding mix**
1 1/2 cups **milk**

Preheat oven to 350 degrees.

In a bowl, mix together cake mix, eggs, and oil until dough forms. Stir in chocolate chips. Spread dough evenly into a lightly greased 9 x 13-inch pan. Bake 14–16 minutes. For a chewy consistency, pull the bars out when the edges are barely starting to turn a light golden brown. With the handle of a wooden spoon, immediately poke holes at 1-inch intervals.

For the topping, in a separate bowl, beat together pudding mix and milk for 2 minutes with a wire whisk. Pour half the pudding over warm bars. Let the rest of the pudding chill and set up 5–10 minutes. Frost the bars with the remaining pudding. Refrigerate at least 1 hour before cutting and serving.

#42

White Chocolate Almond Bars

MAKES 24 BARS

1 box	**yellow or chocolate cake mix**
2	**eggs**
1/2 cup	**butter or margarine, softened**
1 cup	**white chocolate chips**
1/2 to 3/4 cup	**chopped almonds**
	frosting of choice (optional)

Preheat oven to 350 degrees.

In a bowl, mix together cake mix, eggs, and butter. Stir in white chocolate chips and chopped almonds; mixture will be stiff. Press dough into a lightly greased 9 x 13-inch pan. Bake 15–18 minutes for a yellow cake mix and 20 minutes for a chocolate cake mix. Serve warm or at room temperature. Can be topped with favorite frosting, if desired.

#43

Chocolate Cheesecake Bars

MAKES 24 BARS

1 box	**chocolate cake mix**
3	**eggs**
½ cup	**butter or margarine, melted**
1 pound (3.5–4 cups)	**powdered sugar**
1 package (8 ounces)	**cream cheese, softened**
1 teaspoon	**vanilla**

Preheat oven to 350 degrees.

In a bowl, mix together cake mix and 1 egg. Stir in butter. Spread dough evenly into a lightly greased 9 x 13-inch pan.

In a separate bowl, mix together powdered sugar, remaining 2 eggs, cream cheese, and vanilla until smooth. Spread mixture over cake layer. Bake 30–35 minutes.

#44

Hello Dollies

MAKES 24 SERVINGS

½ cup	**butter or margarine**
2 cups	**crushed graham crackers**
1 cup	**chocolate chips**
1 cup	**sweetened coconut flakes**
⅔ cup	**chopped nuts**
1 can (14 ounces)	**sweetened condensed milk**

Preheat oven to 350 degrees.

Melt butter in a glass 9 x 13-inch pan in the oven. Sprinkle graham cracker crumbs over butter. Layer chocolate chips, coconut, and nuts over crust. Drizzle sweetened condensed milk over top. Bake 20 minutes. Cool completely and cut into bars.

#45–54

CAKES & BUNDT CAKES

#45

Double-Chocolate Almond Cake

MAKES 20–24 SERVINGS

1 box	**chocolate cake mix**
	ingredients listed on back of box
1/2 cup	**diced almonds**
3/4 cup	**chocolate chips**

Topping:

1 1/2 cups	**milk**
1 package (8 ounces)	**cream cheese, softened**
1 small box	**chocolate instant pudding mix**
1 container (8 ounces)	**frozen whipped topping, thawed**
1	**chocolate bar, shaved**

Preheat oven to 350 degrees.

Make cake batter according to package directions. Stir almonds and chocolate chips into batter. Pour batter into a greased 9 x 13-inch pan. Bake 30–35 minutes, or until a toothpick inserted in the center comes out clean. Allow cake to cool to room temperature.

For the topping, in a bowl, gradually beat milk into cream cheese. Stir in pudding mix. Spread over cooled cake. Spread whipped topping over top and garnish with chocolate shavings. Refrigerate until ready to serve.

#46

Banana Chocolate Chip Cake

MAKES 12 SERVINGS

2 cups	**flour**
1 teaspoon	**baking soda**
1/4 teaspoon	**salt**
1/2 cup	**butter or margarine, softened**
3/4 cup	**brown sugar**
2 cups	**mashed ripe bananas**
2	**eggs, beaten**
1 cup	**mini chocolate chips**
1/2 container (16 ounces)	**chocolate frosting**

Preheat oven to 350 degrees.

In a bowl, mix together flour, baking soda, and salt.

In a separate large bowl, mix together butter and brown sugar. Stir banana and eggs into butter mixture. Gradually stir in one-third of the flour mixture at a time until flour is blended. Stir in chocolate chips. Pour batter into a greased 8 x 8-inch pan. Bake 32–38 minutes, or until a toothpick inserted in the center comes out clean. Allow cake to cool to room temperature. Frost with chocolate frosting.

#47

Blackberry Chocolate Cake

MAKES 20–24 SERVINGS

1 box	**chocolate cake mix**
3	**eggs**
1 can (21 ounces)	**blackberry pie filling**
1 cup	**chopped nuts**
1 cup	**chocolate chips**
½ cup	**brown sugar**

Preheat oven to 350 degrees.

In a bowl, combine cake mix, eggs, and pie filling. Spread mixture into a greased 9 x 13-inch pan. Sprinkle nuts, chocolate chips, and brown sugar over the top. Bake 30–35 minutes, or until a toothpick inserted in the center comes out clean.

Variation: Strawberry or cherry pie filling can be used in place of blackberry pie filling.

#48

Chocolate Peanut Butter Cake

MAKES 20–24 SERVINGS

1 box	**chocolate cake mix**
	ingredients listed on back of box
½ cup	**chunky peanut butter**
1 cup	**semisweet chocolate chips**

Frosting:

1 container (16 ounces)	**chocolate frosting**
¼ cup	**creamy peanut butter**
½ cup	**chopped peanuts (optional)**

Preheat oven to 350 degrees.

Make batter according to package directions. Mix in peanut butter with a hand mixer. With a spoon, stir in chocolate chips. Pour batter into a greased 9 x 13-inch pan. Bake 25–30 minutes, or until a toothpick inserted in the center comes out clean. Allow cake to cool completely.

For the frosting, in a bowl, mix frosting and peanut butter together. Spread over top of cooled cake. Sprinkle with chopped peanuts, if desired.

#49

Entertaining Delight Cake

MAKES 12 SERVINGS

1 box	**devil's food cake mix**
	ingredients listed on back of box
1 cup	**semisweet chocolate chips**
1 large box	**chocolate instant pudding mix**
	ingredients listed on back of box
1 container (8 ounces)	**frozen whipped topping, thawed**
1	**chocolate bar, shaved**

Preheat oven to 350 degrees.

Make batter according to package directions and mix with a hand mixer for 2 minutes. Stir in chocolate chips. Pour the batter into a greased 9 x 13-inch pan. Bake for the amount of time instructed on the back of the box. Allow cake to cool.

While cake is cooling, make pudding according to package directions. Allow pudding to set up in the refrigerator. Cut the cake into long skinny pieces, about 1½ x 3 inches. Place one slice of cake on a small plate. Place a large scoop of pudding over the cake. Place another slice of cake over the top of pudding. Scoop some more pudding on cake. Top with whipped topping. Sprinkle shaved chocolate over the whipped topping.

#50

Moist Chocolate Mayonnaise Cake

MAKES 16 SERVINGS

1 box	**chocolate cake mix**
4	**eggs**
1 cup	**mayonnaise**
1 cup	**water**
2 cups	**miniature marshmallows**
1 cup	**semisweet or milk chocolate chips**
1 cup	**chopped nuts**
	powdered sugar or chocolate syrup for decorating

Preheat oven to 350 degrees.

In a bowl, mix together cake mix, eggs, mayonnaise, and water with a hand mixer for 2 minutes. Stir in marshmallows, chocolate chips, and nuts. Pour batter into a greased 10-inch fluted-tube pan. Bake 45–50 minutes, or until cake springs back when touched. Remove from oven and let sit 5 minutes.

While still hot, invert onto a serving platter; cool completely. Sprinkle powdered sugar or drizzle chocolate syrup over the top to decorate.

#51

Chocolate Peanut Butter Candy Cake

MAKES 20–24 SERVINGS

1 box	**chocolate cake mix**
	ingredients listed on back of box
1½ cups	**Reese's Pieces, peanut M&M's, or peanut butter M&M's, plus more for serving**
2 teaspoons	**flour**

Frosting:

1 container (16 ounces)	**chocolate frosting**
¼ cup	**creamy peanut butter**

Preheat oven to 350 degrees.

Make batter according to package directions.

In a ziplock bag, shake candy with flour. With a spoon, stir candy into cake batter. Then pour the batter into a greased 9 x 13-inch pan. Bake 30–40 minutes. Allow cake to cool completely.

For the frosting, in a bowl, mix frosting and peanut butter together. Frost cake and serve. For a fun border, place extra candies around the outer edge.

#52

Cherry-Chocolate Bundt Cake

MAKES 16 SERVINGS

1 box	**chocolate cake mix**
3	**eggs**
1 can (21 ounces)	**cherry pie filling**
1 container (16 ounces)	**chocolate frosting or 1 can (21 ounces) cherry pie filling**

Preheat oven to 350 degrees.

In a bowl, mix together cake mix and eggs. Stir in 1 can pie filling until cake mix is completely dissolved into batter. Pour batter into a greased bundt pan. Bake 40–50 minutes, or until a toothpick inserted in the center comes out clean.

While still hot, invert the cake onto a platter. When cool, frost with chocolate frosting or spoon a second can of pie filling over top.

#53

Sweet-Glazed Chocolate Bundt Cake

MAKES 16 SERVINGS

4 eggs
3/4 cup sour cream
1/2 cup water
1/2 cup vegetable oil
1 box white (or chocolate) cake mix
1 small box chocolate instant pudding mix
1 cup chocolate chips

Chocolate Glaze:

3/4 cup semisweet chocolate chips
1 tablespoon corn syrup
3 tablespoons butter or margarine
1/4 teaspoon vanilla

Preheat oven to 350 degrees.

In a large bowl, beat together eggs, sour cream, water, and oil until thoroughly mixed. Stir in cake mix and pudding mix. Fold in chocolate chips. Pour batter into a greased and floured bundt pan. Bake 45–50 minutes, or until a toothpick inserted in the center comes out clean. While still hot, invert the cake onto a platter; allow cake to cool.

For the chocolate glaze, in a heavy saucepan, combine chocolate chips, corn syrup, and butter. Stir over low heat until chocolate is melted; stir in vanilla. Spread warm glaze over top of cake, allowing glaze to drizzle down the sides.

#54

Butterfinger Sheet Cake

MAKES 24–28 SERVINGS

1¼ cups	butter or margarine, divided
½ cup	baking cocoa, divided
1 cup	water
2 cups	flour
1½ cups	brown sugar
1 teaspoon	baking soda
½ teaspoon	salt
1 can (14 ounces)	sweetened condensed milk, divided
2	eggs
1 teaspoon	vanilla
1 cup	powdered sugar
6	fun-size Butterfinger candy bars, crushed

Preheat oven to 350 degrees.

In a small saucepan, melt 1 cup butter. Stir in ¼ cup cocoa and water; bring to a boil. Remove from heat.

In a large bowl, mix together flour, brown sugar, baking soda, and salt. Beat into batter the cocoa mixture, ⅓ cup sweetened condensed milk, eggs, and vanilla until smooth. Pour batter into a greased baking sheet with sides. Bake 15–20 minutes.

Make frosting by combining remaining ¼ cup melted butter, remaining ¼ cup cocoa, and remaining sweetened condensed milk in a bowl; stir in powdered sugar and then spread over warm cake. Sprinkle crushed Butterfinger over top.

Variation: Sprinkle 1 cup sweetened coconut flakes over cake in place of Butterfinger.

#55-64

ICE CREAM CAKES & SANDWICHES

#55

Colorful Ice Cream Sandwiches

MAKES 16–18 ICE CREAM SANDWICHES

1 box	**chocolate or white cake mix**
½ cup	**vegetable oil or butter or margarine, melted**
2	**eggs**
1 to 1½ cups	**plain M&M's**
½ gallon	**vanilla or chocolate ice cream**

Preheat oven to 350 degrees.

In a large bowl, mix together cake mix, oil, and eggs. The dough will be stiff. Mix in M&M's. Using a cookie scoop, drop dough by teaspoonfuls onto a baking sheet. Bake 8–12 minutes. Remove cookies from the oven and allow to set up on hot baking sheet for 3 minutes. Remove from pan and place on nonstick cooling rack to cool. Once completely cooled, place a scoopful of ice cream between two cookies. Wrap the sandwiches in plastic wrap. Store cookies in an airtight container in the freezer.

#56

Grasshopper Ice Cream Sandwiches

MAKES 16–18 ICE CREAM SANDWICHES

1 box	**chocolate cake mix**
½ cup	**butter or margarine, softened**
2	**eggs**
1 cup	**green mint chips**
½ gallon	**mint chocolate chip ice cream**

Preheat oven to 350 degrees.

In a large bowl, mix together cake mix, butter, and eggs. The dough will be stiff. Mix in mint chips. Using a cookie scoop, drop dough by teaspoonfuls onto a baking sheet. Bake 8–12 minutes. Remove cookies from oven and allow to set up on hot baking sheet for 2–3 minutes. Remove from pan and place on nonstick cooling rack to cool. Once completely cooled, place a scoopful of ice cream between two cookies. Wrap the sandwiches in plastic wrap. Store cookies in an airtight container in the freezer.

#57

Nutty Chocolate Chip Ice Cream Sandwiches

MAKES 16–18 ICE CREAM SANDWICHES

1 box	**white cake mix**
½ cup	**butter or margarine, softened**
2	**eggs**
1 cup	**semisweet or milk chocolate chips**
½ cup	**chopped nuts**
½ gallon	**chocolate ice cream**

Preheat oven to 350 degrees.

In a large bowl, mix together cake mix, butter, and eggs. The dough will be stiff. Mix in chocolate chips and nuts. Using a cookie scoop, drop dough by teaspoonfuls onto a baking sheet. Bake 8–12 minutes. Remove cookies from oven and allow to set up on hot baking sheet for 2–3 minutes. Remove from pan and place on nonstick cooling rack to cool. Once completely cooled, place a scoopful of ice cream between two cookies. Wrap the sandwiches in plastic wrap. Store cookies in an airtight container in the freezer.

#58

Brownie Ice Cream Cake

MAKES 20 SERVINGS

1 box	**chocolate cake mix**
½ cup	**butter or margarine, melted**
1	**egg**
½ cup	**chopped or grated nuts**
1½ boxes (½ gallon each)	**vanilla or fudge ripple ice cream, softened**
1 jar (11.75 ounces)	**fudge ice cream topping**
	chocolate chips or chopped nuts (optional)

Preheat oven to 350 degrees.

In a bowl, mix together cake mix, butter, and egg. Stir in nuts. Press dough evenly into a lightly greased 9 x 13-inch pan. Bake 10–12 minutes, or until a toothpick inserted in the center comes out clean. With a fork, remove the air pockets by pushing down evenly over the entire hot crust. Allow crust to cool completely.

Spread softened ice cream evenly over crust. Spread ice cream topping evenly over ice cream. Sprinkle chocolate chips or nuts over top, if desired. Cover and freeze at least 4 hours before serving.

#59

Instant Ice Cream Sandwich Cake

MAKES 20 SERVINGS

1 jar (16 ounces)	**chocolate syrup**
3/4 cup	**peanut butter**
19	**ice cream sandwiches**
1 container (12 ounces)	**frozen whipped topping, thawed**
1 1/4 cups	**chopped salted peanuts, divided**

Heat chocolate syrup for 2 minutes in the microwave. Stir peanut butter into hot syrup; allow to cool. Line the bottom of a 9 x 13-inch glass pan with a layer of ice cream sandwiches. Spread half the chocolate mixture over sandwiches. Cover with half the whipped topping. Sprinkle 1/2 cup peanuts over top. Repeat with another layer of ice cream sandwiches, remaining chocolate mixture, remaining whipped topping, and remaining nuts. Freeze 1 hour or more until ready to serve.

#60

Cookie Dough Ice Cream Cake

MAKES 20 SERVINGS

1 box	**chocolate, yellow, or white cake mix**
½ cup	**butter or margarine, melted**
1	**egg**
1½ cups	**mini chocolate chips, divided**
1½ boxes (½ gallon each)	**chocolate chip cookie dough ice cream, softened**
1 jar (11.75 ounces)	**fudge or caramel ice cream topping**

Preheat oven to 350 degrees.

In a bowl, mix together cake mix, butter, and egg. Stir in 1 cup chocolate chips. Press dough evenly into a lightly greased 9 x 13-inch pan. Bake 10–12 minutes. Crust will still be doughy. With a fork, remove the air pockets by pushing down evenly over the entire hot crust; allow crust to cool completely.

Open ice cream boxes so they lay flat and cut softened ice cream into equal-size slices. Spread half the ice cream evenly over crust. Spread fudge or caramel over the first layer of ice cream. Spread remaining ice cream slices over top. Sprinkle remaining ½ cup chocolate chips over top. Cover and freeze at least 4 hours before serving.

#61

Cookies-and-Cream Ice Cream Cake

MAKES 20 SERVINGS

1 box	**chocolate or white cake mix**
½ cup	**butter or margarine, melted**
1	**egg**
1½ boxes (½ gallon each)	**cookies-and-cream ice cream, softened**
1 jar (11.75 ounces)	**fudge ice cream topping**
2 cups	**chopped chocolate sandwich cookies, divided**

Preheat oven to 350 degrees.

In a bowl, mix together cake mix, butter, and egg. Press dough evenly into a lightly greased 9 x 13-inch pan. Bake 10–12 minutes. Crust will still be doughy. With a fork, remove the air pockets by pushing down evenly over the entire hot crust; allow crust to cool completely.

Open ice cream boxes so they lay flat and cut softened ice cream into equal-size slices. Spread half the ice cream evenly over crust. Soften fudge in microwave if needed and then drizzle evenly over ice cream. Sprinkle 1 cup chopped cookies over fudge. Spread remaining ice cream sliced over cookie layer. Sprinkle remaining 1 cup chopped cookies over top. Cover and freeze at least 4 hours before serving.

#62

Mint Chocolate Chip Ice Cream Cake

MAKES 20 SERVINGS

1 box	**chocolate cake mix**
$\frac{1}{2}$ cup	**butter or margarine, melted**
1	**egg**
$1\frac{1}{2}$ to 2 boxes ($\frac{1}{2}$ gallon each)	**mint chocolate chip ice cream, softened**
1 jar (11.75 ounces)	**fudge ice cream topping**

Preheat oven to 350 degrees.

In a bowl, mix together cake mix, butter, and egg. Press dough evenly into a lightly greased 9 x 13-inch pan. Bake 10–12 minutes. Crust will still be doughy. With a fork, remove the air pockets by pushing down evenly over the entire hot crust; allow crust to cool completely.

Open ice cream boxes so they lay flat and cut softened ice cream into equal-size slices. Spread ice cream evenly over crust. Drizzle ice cream topping evenly over ice cream. Cover and freeze at least 4 hours before serving.

#63

Peanut Butter Chocolate Ice Cream Cake

MAKES 20 SERVINGS

1 box	**chocolate cake mix**
½ cup	**butter or margarine, melted**
1	**egg**
¾ cup	**peanut butter chips**
1½ to 2 boxes (½ gallon each)	**chocolate or peanut butter chocolate ice cream**
⅔ cup	**peanut butter, softened**
1 cup	**corn syrup**
¾ cup	**chopped peanuts (optional)**

Preheat oven to 350 degrees.

In a bowl, mix together cake mix, butter, and egg. Stir in peanut butter chips. Press dough evenly into a lightly greased 9 x 13-inch pan. Bake 10–12 minutes. Crust will still be doughy. With a fork, remove the air pockets by pushing down evenly over the entire hot crust; allow crust to cool completely.

Open ice cream boxes so they lay flat and cut softened ice cream into equal-size slices. Spread ice cream evenly over crust. Soften peanut butter in microwave for 10–30 seconds on high. Stir in corn syrup. Pour topping over the ice cream. Sprinkle chopped peanuts over top, if desired. Cover and freeze at least 4 hours before serving.

#64

Rocky Road Ice Cream Cake

MAKES 20 SERVINGS

1 box	**chocolate or white cake mix**
½ cup	**butter or margarine**
1	**egg**
1½ to 2 boxes (½ gallon each)	**rocky road ice cream, softened**
1 jar (11.75 ounces)	**marshmallow or fudge ice cream topping**
½ cup	**chopped nuts**
½ cup	**mini chocolate chips**
¾ cup	**miniature marshmallows**

Preheat oven to 350 degrees.

In a bowl, mix together cake mix, butter, and egg. Press dough evenly into a lightly greased 9 x 13-inch pan. Bake 10–12 minutes. Crust will still be doughy. With a fork, remove the air pockets by pushing down evenly over the entire hot crust; allow crust to cool completely.

Open ice cream boxes so they lay flat and cut softened ice cream into equal-size slices. Spread ice cream evenly over crust. Microwave ice cream topping 15–20 seconds, stir, and spread evenly over ice cream. Sprinkle nuts, chocolate chips, and marshmallows over top. Cover and freeze at least 4 hours or overnight.

Variation: Vanilla or chocolate ice cream can be substituted for rocky road ice cream.

#65–74

CHEESECAKES, DESSERT PIZZAS & PIES

#65

Candy Bar Cheesecake

MAKES 10–12 SERVINGS

1½ cups	**crushed chocolate sandwich cookies**
4 tablespoons	**butter or margarine, melted**
3 packages (8 ounces each)	**cream cheese, softened**
¾ cup	**sugar**
1½ teaspoons	**vanilla**
3	**eggs**
4	**Snickers candy bars, chilled and thinly sliced, divided**
1 bag (11.5 ounces)	**chocolate chips**
1 tablespoon	**shortening or butter**

Preheat oven to 300 degrees.

In a small bowl, combine cookie crumbs and butter and press over bottom and up the sides of a 9-inch springform pan.

In a large bowl, beat together cream cheese, sugar, and vanilla. Beat in eggs one at a time until smooth; fold in 3 sliced candy bars. Pour cream cheese mixture over crust. Bake 1 hour. Turn off oven without opening the door and leave cheesecake in oven 1 hour more.

Melt chocolate chips and shortening or butter together in the microwave 45–60 seconds; stir until smooth. Spread chocolate over cheesecake. Refrigerate 6 hours or overnight. Arrange remaining candy bar slices over top.

#66

Chocolate Chip Cheesecake

MAKES 10–12 SERVINGS

1½ cups	**chocolate graham cracker crumbs**
¼ cup	**sugar**
⅓ cup	**butter or margarine, melted**
3 packages (8 ounces each)	**cream cheese, softened**
2 teaspoons	**vanilla**
3	**eggs**
1 can (14 ounces)	**sweetened condensed milk**
1½ cups	**mini semisweet chocolate chips, divided**
1 teaspoon	**flour**

Preheat oven to 300 degrees.

In a small bowl, combine graham cracker crumbs, sugar, and butter. Press over bottom and up the sides of a 9-inch springform pan.

In a large bowl, beat together cream cheese and vanilla. Beat in eggs one at a time until smooth. Slowly mix in sweetened condensed milk. Toss ½ cup mini chocolate chips with flour. Fold coated chocolate chips into cream cheese mixture. Pour mixture into crust. Bake 1 hour. Turn off oven without opening the door and leave cheesecake in oven 1 hour more.

Remove from oven and sprinkle remaining 1 cup mini chocolate chips over top. Refrigerate 6–8 hours or overnight.

#67

Fudge Truffle Cheesecake

MAKES 10–12 SERVINGS

1½ cups	vanilla wafer crumbs
½ cup	powdered sugar
⅓ cup	baking cocoa
½ cup	butter or margarine, melted
3 packages (8 ounces each)	cream cheese, softened
1 can (14 ounces)	sweetened condensed milk
4	eggs
1½ teaspoons	vanilla
1 bag (11.5 ounces)	semisweet chocolate chips

Preheat oven to 300 degrees.

In a bowl, combine wafer crumbs, powdered sugar, cocoa, and butter. Press mixture into the bottom of a greased 9-inch springform pan.

In a large bowl, beat cream cheese, sweetened condensed milk, eggs, and vanilla together until smooth.

In a heavy 1½-quart saucepan, melt chocolate chips, stirring constantly. Stir melted chocolate into cream cheese mixture. Pour chocolate cream cheese mixture over crust. Bake 1 hour. Turn off oven without opening the door and leave cheesecake in oven 1 hour more. Refrigerate 3–4 hours or overnight.

#68

Chocolate Strawberry Cheesecake Bars

MAKES 20–24 SERVINGS

1 box	**chocolate cake mix**
½ cup	**butter or margarine, melted**
1	**egg**
1 jar (18 ounces)	**seedless strawberry jam, divided**
2 packages (8 ounces each)	**cream cheese, softened**
¾ cup	**sugar**
½ teaspoon	**vanilla**
3	**eggs**
	chocolate syrup

Preheat oven to 350 degrees.

In a bowl, mix together cake mix, butter, and egg. Spread dough evenly into a greased 9 x 13-inch pan. Stir jam until smooth then spread 1 cup jam evenly over crust.

In a separate bowl, mix together cream cheese, sugar, and vanilla. Beat in eggs one at a time. Pour over the jam layer. Bake 30 minutes, or until cheesecake is set and firm in the center; remove from oven and allow to cool.

In a saucepan, warm 1 cup jam over medium heat. Drizzle jam evenly over cooled cheesecake. Refrigerate 2–3 hours or overnight. To decorate, drizzle chocolate syrup over top before cutting into bars and serving.

#69

Banana Split Pizza

MAKES 24–28 SERVINGS

1 box	chocolate cake mix
2	eggs
1/2 cup	vegetable oil or butter or margarine, melted
1/4 cup	powdered sugar
1 package (8 ounces)	cream cheese, softened
1 container (8 ounces)	frozen whipped topping, thawed
1 can (8 ounces)	pineapple chunks, drained
2	bananas, thinly sliced
3/4 cup	chopped peanuts or almonds
1 1/2 cups	sliced strawberries
	chocolate syrup (optional)

Preheat oven to 350 degrees.

In a bowl, mix together cake mix, eggs, and oil until cake mix is completely worked into the dough. Spread the dough thinly to cover a jellyroll pan or baking sheet. Bake 12 minutes, or until crust begins to crack and appears to be done; cool completely.

In a separate bowl, mix together powdered sugar, cream cheese, and whipped topping. Spread over crust. Top evenly with fruit and nuts. Drizzle chocolate syrup over the top to decorate, if desired. Serve immediately.

#70

Chocolate Chip Cookie Pizza

MAKES 24–28 SERVINGS

1 box	**yellow or white cake mix**
½ cup	**butter or margarine, melted**
2	**eggs**
1 cup	**semisweet or milk chocolate chips**
1½ cups	**milk**
1 small box	**chocolate instant pudding mix**
½ cup	**plain yogurt**
⅓ cup	**peanut butter**
	sliced bananas, sweetened coconut flakes, chocolate chips, peanuts, miniature marshmallows, or chopped candy bars

Preheat oven to 350 degrees.

In a bowl, mix together cake mix, butter, and eggs until cake mix is completely worked into the dough; stir in chocolate chips. Spread the dough thinly to cover a jellyroll pan or baking sheet. Bake 10–12 minutes, or until done; allow to cool completely.

In a separate bowl, mix together milk, pudding mix, yogurt, and peanut butter until smooth and thick. Chill 5–10 minutes, or until pudding mixture sets; spread over crust. Sprinkle your favorite toppings over top. Refrigerate before and after serving.

#71

Coconut Almond Pizza

MAKES 24–28 SERVINGS

1 box	**chocolate cake mix**
2	**eggs**
½ cup	**butter or margarine, melted**
1 can (14 ounces)	**sweetened condensed milk**
¾ cup	**sliced almonds**
1 cup	**sweetened coconut flakes**
1 cup	**semisweet chocolate chips**
2½ tablespoons	**milk**

Preheat oven to 350 degrees.

In a bowl, mix together cake mix, eggs, and butter until cake mix is completely worked into the dough. Spread dough thinly to cover a jellyroll pan or baking sheet. Bake 12 minutes, or until crust begins to crack and appears to be done; cool completely. Pour sweetened condensed milk evenly over crust. Sprinkle almonds and coconut over top.

In a saucepan, melt chocolate chips and milk together until smooth. Drizzle chocolate over pizza.

#72

Candy Bar Pudding Pie

MAKES 6–8 SERVINGS

2	**Snickers bars, cut into $\frac{1}{2}$-inch pieces, divided**
1 (6-ounce)	**ready-made chocolate crumb crust**
$1\frac{3}{4}$ cups	**milk**
1 small box	**chocolate instant pudding mix**

Sprinkle three-fourths of the candy bar pieces into pie crust.

In a bowl, whisk together milk and pudding mix until pudding begins to thicken. Spread pudding into pie crust. Refrigerate pie at least 1 hour, or until ready to serve. Sprinkle remaining candy bar pieces over top.

Variations: Try using peanut butter cups, Baby Ruth candy bars, or other favorite candy bars in place of Snickers.

#73

Chocolate Mousse Pie

MAKES 6–8 SERVINGS

1 package (8 ounces)	**cream cheese, softened**
$\frac{1}{2}$ cup	**sugar**
1 teaspoon	**vanilla**
$\frac{1}{3}$ cup	**baking cocoa**
$\frac{1}{3}$ cup	**milk**
1 container (8 ounces)	**frozen whipped topping, thawed**
1 (6-ounce)	**ready-made chocolate crumb crust**
	mini chocolate chips (optional)

In a large bowl, mix together cream cheese, sugar, and vanilla until smooth; stir in cocoa and milk. Fold in whipped topping and then spoon filling into pie crust. Freeze 6 hours or overnight. Garnish with mini chocolate chips, if desired.

#74

Cookies-and-Cream Ice Cream Pie

MAKES 6–8 SERVINGS

½ gallon	**cookies-and-cream ice cream, softened**
1 (6-ounce)	**ready-made chocolate crumb crust**
5 to 7	**chocolate sandwich cookies, crumbled**
	whipped topping (optional)

Spoon and spread ice cream into pie crust. Freeze 1 hour or more before serving. Sprinkle crumbled cookies over top. Garnish with whipped topping, if desired.

Variations: Use cookie dough ice cream and sprinkle ½ cup mini chocolate chips over top. Use any type of candy bar ice cream and sprinkle 1 chopped candy bar over top.

#75–89

FAMILY FAVORITES

#75

Hot Chocolate

MAKES 8 SERVINGS

¼ cup	cocoa powder
½ cup	sugar
⅓ cup	water
dash	salt
8 cups	milk
1 teaspoon	vanilla
	whipped topping or mini marshmallows for garnish (optional)

In a 3-quart saucepan, combine cocoa, sugar, water, and salt; bring to a boil. Stir in milk and cook over medium heat until hot; stir in vanilla. Pour into eight glasses. Garnish with whipped topping or mini marshmallows, if desired.

Variations: Add 1 teaspoon amaretto flavoring or mint extract instead of vanilla.

#76

Cookies-and-Cream Milkshakes

MAKES 4 SHAKES

½ box (½ gallon)	**vanilla ice cream**
8	**double-stuffed chocolate sandwich cookies, broken, plus more for garnish**
1 to 1½ cups	**milk**

Combine all ingredients in the blender and blend for 30–60 seconds. For thicker shakes, use 1 cup milk. For thinner shakes, use 1½ cups milk. Garnish each shake with extra crumbled sandwich cookies.

#77

No-Bake Peanut Butter Oatmeal Squares

MAKES 24 SQUARES

2 cups	**sugar**
¼ cup	**baking cocoa**
½ cup	**milk**
½ cup	**butter or margarine**
1 teaspoon	**vanilla**
1 pinch	**salt**
½ cup	**chunky peanut butter**
3¼ cups	**quick oats**

In a 3-quart heavy saucepan, combine sugar, cocoa, milk, and butter. Bring to a boil, stirring occasionally; boil 1–1½ minutes. Remove from heat and stir in vanilla, salt, and peanut butter; fold in oats until covered. Spoon mixture into a buttered 9 x 13-inch pan. Chill 30 minutes and then cut into squares. Store leftovers in an airtight container.

#78

Chocolate Cream Cheese Cupcakes

MAKES AT LEAST 24 CUPCAKES

1 box	**devil's food or German chocolate cake mix**
	ingredients listed on back of box
1 package (8 ounces)	**cream cheese, softened**
1	**egg**
$\frac{1}{3}$ cup	**sugar**
1 cup	**semisweet or milk chocolate chips**
1 container (16 ounces)	**chocolate or white frosting**

Preheat oven to 350 degrees.

Mix cake batter according to package directions until smooth. Place paper cupcake liners in muffin pan. Fill muffin cups half full with batter.

In a separate bowl, combine cream cheese, egg, and sugar until smooth. Stir in chocolate chips. Place a tablespoon of cream filling in the center of each cupcake. Bake 18–22 minutes. Remove cupcakes from pan and cool completely. Top with frosting.

Variation: Butterscotch or peanut butter chips can be substituted for chocolate chips.

#79

Chocolate Peanut Butter Surprise Cupcakes

MAKES 24 CUPCAKES

1 box	**chocolate cake mix**
	ingredients listed on back of box
1 cup	**peanut butter chips**
24	**bite-size Snickers or miniature peanut butter cups, unwrapped**
1 container (16 ounces)	**chocolate frosting**

Preheat oven to 350 degrees.

Mix cake batter according to package directions until smooth. With a spoon, fold in the peanut butter chips. Place paper cupcake liners in muffin pan. Fill muffin cups one-third full. Bake 7–8 minutes.

Place candy in center of each cupcake. Top candy with cake batter to fill muffin cups three-fourths full. Bake an additional 15–18 minutes, or until the top springs back when touched. Remove from pan and allow to cool completely. Top cupcakes with frosting.

#80

Chocolate-Covered Cereal Squares

MAKES 24 SQUARES

1 cup	**sugar**
½ cup	**corn syrup**
1 teaspoon	**vanilla**
¾ cup	**creamy peanut butter**
4½ cups	**corn flakes**
1 bag (11.5 ounces)	**chocolate chips**
2 tablespoons	**milk**

In a nonstick 3- to 4-quart pan, bring sugar and corn syrup to a boil. Boil until sugar dissolves. Stir in vanilla and peanut butter until smooth; remove from heat. Fold in corn flakes until evenly coated. Spread into a greased 9 x 13-inch pan.

In a saucepan, melt chocolate chips and milk together, stirring constantly until smooth. Spread melted chocolate over cereal layer; cut into bars. Serve chilled or at room temperature.

#81

Butterscotch Chocolate Crispy Squares

MAKES 16 SQUARES

1 cup	**butterscotch chips**
½ cup	**peanut butter**
4 cups	**crispy rice cereal**
1 cup	**chocolate chips**
1 tablespoon	**water**
½ cup	**powdered sugar**
2 tablespoons	**butter or margarine**

In a saucepan, melt butterscotch chips and peanut butter together. Stir in cereal. Press half the cereal mixture into a lightly greased 9 x 9-inch pan.

In a separate saucepan, combine chocolate chips, water, powdered sugar, and butter over low heat. Stir occasionally until chocolate is melted. Pour chocolate mixture evenly over cereal layer. Press the remaining cereal mixture on top. Chill 1 hour or until set. Allow bars to come to room temperature before cutting them to serve.

#82

Chocolate Lush

MAKES 20–24 SERVINGS

1 cup	**butter or margarine, softened**
1 cup	**flour**
½ cup	**chopped nuts (optional)**
1 package (8 ounces)	**cream cheese, softened**
1 cup	**powdered sugar**
1 container (12 ounces)	**frozen whipped topping, thawed and divided**
2 small boxes	**chocolate instant pudding mix**
3 cups	**milk**

Preheat oven to 350 degrees.

Combine butter, flour, and nuts, if desired, with pastry blender until crumbly. Press mixture into a glass 9 x 13-inch pan. Bake 10 minutes; cool completely.

In a bowl, mix together cream cheese and powdered sugar. Fold in 1 cup whipped topping. Spread cream cheese mixture over cooled crust. Mix together pudding mixes and milk until pudding starts to thicken. Pour pudding over cream cheese layer. Spread remaining whipped topping over top. Refrigerate at least 1 hour, or until ready to serve.

#83

Graham Cracker Chocolate Squares

MAKES 16 SQUARES

2 cups	**graham cracker crumbs**
2 cups	**sweetened coconut flakes**
1/4 cup	**butter or margarine, melted**
1 can (14 ounces)	**sweetened condensed milk**
1 cup	**chocolate chips**

Preheat oven to 400 degrees.

In a large bowl, combine all ingredients. Spread mixture into a greased 8 x 8-inch pan. Bake 15 minutes and cool 5 minutes; cut into squares and serve warm.

#84

Peanut Butter Chocolate Crispy Treats

MAKES 24 BARS

1 cup	**creamy peanut butter**
4 tablespoons	**butter or margarine**
1 bag (16 ounces)	**miniature marshmallows**
7 cups	**crispy rice cereal**
1 bag (11.5 ounces)	**milk chocolate chips**
2 tablespoons	**milk**

In a 3- to 4-quart pan, melt peanut butter and butter together until smooth. Stir marshmallows into peanut butter mixture until melted. Fold in cereal until evenly coated. Press cereal mixture into a lightly buttered 9 x 13-inch pan.

In a small heavy saucepan, melt chocolate chips and milk together until smooth. Spread chocolate evenly over cereal layer. Chill in refrigerator 1–2 hours, or until chocolate is hard.

#85

Chocolate Chip Banana Bread

MAKES 10–12 SERVINGS

½ cup	**butter or margarine, softened**
¾ cup	**brown sugar**
2	**eggs, beaten**
2 cups	**mashed overripe bananas**
1½ teaspoons	**pumpkin pie spice**
2 cups	**flour**
1 teaspoon	**baking soda**
¼ teaspoon	**salt**
1 cup	**chocolate chips**

Preheat oven to 350 degrees.

In a large bowl, combine butter and brown sugar. Stir in eggs, bananas, and pumpkin pie spice.

In a separate bowl, combine flour, baking soda, and salt. Slowly stir flour mixture into banana mixture until just moistened; fold in chocolate chips. Pour batter into a greased 5 x 9-inch loaf pan. Bake 50–55 minutes, or until bread springs back when touched in center. Allow bread to cool in pan 10 minutes before inverting onto a serving platter or wire rack.

#86

Oatmeal Caramelitos

MAKES 28–32 BARS

2 cups	**flour**
1½ cups	**brown sugar**
½ teaspoon	**salt**
2 cups	**oats**
1 teaspoon	**baking powder**
1½ cups	**butter or margarine, softened**
1 package (11.5 ounces)	**milk chocolate chips**
1 cup	**chopped nuts**
2 jars (12.25 ounces each)	**caramel ice cream topping**

Preheat oven to 350 degrees.

In a bowl, combine flour, brown sugar, salt, oats, and baking powder. Using a fork or pastry cutter, cut butter into flour mixture until crumbly. Press half the mixture into a lightly greased jelly roll pan or baking sheet. Bake 10 minutes. Remove from oven and immediately sprinkle chocolate chips over top. Allow chocolate to melt and spread evenly over top. Sprinkle nuts over chocolate layer. Pour caramel over chocolate and nuts. Sprinkle remaining oat crumbs over caramel. Bake 15–20 minutes; cool completely before serving.

#87

Peanut Butter Chocolate Squares

MAKES 30–40 SQUARES

2 ½ cups	**graham cracker crumbs***
1 cup	**creamy peanut butter**
2 ¾ cups	**powdered sugar**
1 cup	**butter or margarine, melted**
1 cup	**semisweet chocolate chips**
1 cup	**milk chocolate chips**

In a bowl, combine graham cracker crumbs, peanut butter, powdered sugar, and butter. Press mixture into a glass 9 x 13-inch pan.

Over a double boiler or in the microwave, melt chocolate chips. Spread melted chocolate over peanut butter layer. Allow chocolate to harden before cutting into bars. (Speed up the hardening process by placing bars in the refrigerator or freezer. Just make sure to allow bars to return to room temperature before cutting or the chocolate top will crack.)

*15 whole graham crackers broken and crumbled equals approximately 2 ½ cups.

#88

Chocolate Pudding–Filled Donuts

MAKES 25–30 DONUTS

2½ tablespoons	**active dry yeast**
½ cup	**warm water**
1 cup	**unseasoned mashed potatoes**
2 cups	**warm milk**
½ cup	**shortening or butter**
1 cup	**sugar**
3	**eggs**
1½ teaspoons	**salt**
6 cups	**flour**
1 small box	**chocolate instant pudding mix**
2 cups	**milk**
	vegetable oil, for frying
1 container (16 ounces)	**chocolate frosting**

In a bowl, mix yeast, water, mashed potatoes, and milk together.

In a separate bowl, combine shortening or butter, sugar, eggs, and salt. Stir mashed potato mixture into bowl with egg mixture. Stir in flour 1 cup at a time. Knead dough 1–2 minutes. Cover bowl with plastic wrap and allow dough to rise 45 minutes.

In a bowl, mix together pudding mix and milk until pudding thickens. Place in the refrigerator until ready to fill donuts.

Roll out dough to 1-inch thickness on a floured cutting board. Cut dough into 4 x 4-inch squares. Fry dough in hot oil. Turn once making sure donut is golden brown on both sides. Spread chocolate frosting over hot donuts and then fill donuts with chocolate pudding using a kitchen syringe. Refrigerate any leftovers.

#89

Chocolate Graham Cracker Cake

MAKES 20 SERVINGS

2 small boxes	**chocolate instant pudding mix**
3 cups	**milk**
1 container (8 ounces)	**frozen whipped topping, thawed**
1 box (14 to 16 ounces)	**graham crackers**
1 container (16 ounces)	**chocolate frosting**

In a 2-quart bowl, combine pudding mix and milk until smooth. Fold in whipped topping. Cover the bottom of a 9 x 13-inch pan with a layer of graham crackers, breaking to fit if necessary. Evenly spread half the pudding mixture over graham crackers. Lay another layer of crackers over pudding mixture. Spread remaining pudding over second graham cracker layer. Top with final layer of graham crackers. Melt chocolate frosting in the microwave 30 seconds. Stir and carefully drizzle chocolate frosting covering the entire cake. Cover and refrigerate a minimum of 3 hours before serving.

Variations: Use vanilla, cheesecake, or white chocolate instant pudding mix in place of chocolate pudding mix.

#90-101

TRIFLES & ENTERTAINING IDEAS

#90

Cookies-and-Cream Trifle

MAKES 24 SERVINGS

1 box	**chocolate or white cake mix**
	ingredients listed on back of box
2 small boxes	**chocolate instant pudding mix**
3 cups	**milk**
1 package (8 ounces)	**cream cheese, softened**
1 package (1 pound)	**chocolate sandwich cookies, chopped**
1 container (12 ounces)	**frozen whipped topping, thawed**

Preheat oven to 350 degrees.

Make and bake cake according to package directions. Allow cake to cool and then crumble it. Mix together pudding mixes and milk and then beat in cream cheese.

In a glass punch bowl, layer half the cake crumbs, half the pudding mixture, and one-third of the cookies. Repeat layers with remaining cake crumbs, pudding mixture, and another third of the cookies. Spread whipped topping over top. Sprinkle remaining third of the cookies over top. Refrigerate until ready to serve.

#91

Mint Brownie Trifle

MAKES 12–15 SERVINGS

1 box (9 x 13-inch family size)	**brownie mix**
	ingredients listed on back of box
1 large box	**vanilla instant pudding mix**
3 cups	**milk**
1 package (18 ounces)	**mint chocolate cookies, crushed**
½ jar (11.75 ounces)	**hot fudge ice cream topping**
1 container (8 ounces)	**frozen whipped topping, thawed**

Preheat oven to 325 degrees.

Prepare and bake brownies according to package directions in a greased 9 x 13-inch pan; cool completely and then cut into tiny squares.

In a bowl, mix pudding with milk until set. Spoon half the pudding into the bottom of a large glass salad bowl or punch bowl. Place half the brownie squares evenly over pudding. Sprinkle one-third of the cookies over brownies. Drizzle half the ice cream topping over cookies. Repeat layers with remaining pudding, brownie squares, and another third of the cookie crumbs. Drizzle remaining ice cream topping over cookies and then spread whipped topping over top. To garnish, sprinkle remaining third of the cookie crumbs over whipped topping.

#92

Butterfinger Brownie à la Mode

MAKES 9 SERVINGS

1 box (8 x 8-inch size)	**brownie mix**
	ingredients listed on back of box
4	**Butterfinger candy bars, chopped and divided**
½ box (½ gallon)	**vanilla ice cream**
	chocolate syrup

Preheat oven to 325 degrees.

Make brownie batter according to package directions. Stir half the chopped Butterfingers into batter. Bake brownies according to package directions.

Place warm brownies on individual serving plates. Place a large scoop of vanilla ice cream over each brownie. Drizzle chocolate syrup over ice cream and then sprinkle with remaining Butterfingers.

#93

Mint Chocolate Chip Brownie Sundaes

MAKES 20–24 SERVINGS

1 box (9 x 13-inch family size)	**brownie mix**
	ingredients listed on back of box
$^3/_4$ cup	**mint chocolate chips**
	chocolate syrup
1 box ($^1/_2$ gallon)	**mint chocolate chip ice cream**

Preheat oven to 325 degrees.

Make brownie batter according to package directions. Stir chocolate chips into batter, and then bake as directed.

In separate serving bowls, drizzle syrup over bottom of dish and place a warm brownie over the syrup. Place one or two scoops of ice cream over top. Drizzle more syrup over ice cream. Serve immediately garnished with whipped topping and mint chocolate chips, if desired.

Variation: For peanut butter sundaes, substitute peanut butter chips and peanut butter ice cream in place of the mint chocolate chips and ice cream.

#94

Raspberry Brownie Cups

MAKES 45–48 CUPS

1 box (9 x 13-inch family size)	**brownie mix**
	ingredients listed on back of box
2 squares (1 ounce each)	**white chocolate for baking**
2 tablespoons	**milk**
1 package (8 ounces)	**cream cheese, softened**
1/4 cup	**powdered sugar**
1 cup	**frozen whipped topping, thawed**
45 to 48	**raspberries**

Preheat oven to 325 degrees.

Make brownie batter according to package directions for cake-like brownies. Place a teaspoon of batter in each cup of a greased mini-muffin pan. Bake 14 minutes. Using a tart shaper or spoon, press down to form hollow brownie cups to hold filling.

In a bowl, melt chocolate and milk together 45–60 seconds in the microwave. Stir until chocolate is completely melted.

In a separate bowl, combine cream cheese and powdered sugar. Gradually stir in melted chocolate. Fold whipped topping into cream cheese mixture. Spoon cream cheese mixture into brownie cups. Place a raspberry on top of each brownie cup. Refrigerate 1–2 hours before serving.

#95

Peanut Butter Chocolate Lush

MAKES 20 SERVINGS

1 box	chocolate cake mix
½ cup	butter or margarine, melted
1	egg
2 small boxes	chocolate instant pudding mix
3 cups	cold milk

Peanut Butter Layer:

⅓ cup	creamy peanut butter
¼ cup	cold milk
1 container (12 ounces)	frozen whipped topping, thawed
	unsalted peanuts
	chocolate syrup

Preheat oven to 350 degrees.

In a bowl, mix together cake mix, butter, and egg. Press dough to cover the bottom of a lightly greased 9 x 13-inch pan. Bake 14–16 minutes. With a fork, remove the air pockets by pushing down evenly over the entire hot crust; cool completely.

Beat together pudding mixes and milk with a wire whisk for 2 minutes. Spread evenly over cooled crust.

For the peanut butter layer, in a separate bowl, mix peanut butter and cold milk together with a wire whisk. Gently stir in whipped topping; spread evenly over chocolate layer. Chill 3–4 hours. To garnish, sprinkle peanuts and drizzle chocolate syrup lightly over the top before serving.

#96

Peanut Butter Cookie Cups

MAKES 32 SERVINGS

1 package (17.5 ounces)	**peanut butter cookie mix**
	ingredients listed on back of package
1 bag (12 ounces)	**miniature peanut butter cups**

Preheat oven to 350 degrees.

Make cookie dough according to package directions. Drop teaspoons of dough into cups of a greased mini-muffin pan. Press an unwrapped miniature peanut butter cup down into the center of each ball of dough until top of chocolate candy is even with top of cookie dough. Bake 8 minutes, or until lightly golden around the edges. Do not overcook. Remove from oven and allow cookies to set up in pan before removing.

Variation: A chocolate chip cookie mix can be used in place of the peanut butter cookie mix.

#97

Chocolate Lovers Parfaits

MAKES 12 LARGE PARFAITS

1 box	**devil's food cake mix**
2	**eggs**
½ cup	**butter or margarine, softened**
1 cup	**semisweet chocolate chips**
2 small boxes	**chocolate instant pudding mix**
4 cups	**milk**
1 container (16 ounces)	**frozen whipped topping, thawed**
	grated chocolate bar (optional)

Preheat oven to 350 degrees.

In a bowl, mix together cake mix, eggs, and butter; stir in chocolate chips. Mixture will be stiff. Press dough into a greased 9 x 13-inch pan. Bake 18 minutes. Allow to cool 1–2 hours and then crumble the cookie bars into a bowl.

In a separate bowl, stir pudding mix and milk together; chill 5 minutes. Layer cookie bar crumbs, pudding, and whipped topping in parfait glasses. Repeat with three layers. Sprinkle grated chocolate over the top of each parfait to garnish, if desired.

#98

Chocolate-Dipped Strawberries

MAKES 10–12 SERVINGS

1 bag (11.5 ounces)	**semisweet or milk chocolate chips**
2 tablespoons	**shortening or butter**
2 pounds	**fresh strawberries**

In a small slow cooker, melt chocolate chips with shortening or butter on high heat. Turn heat to low.

Wash strawberries with leaves on. Place strawberries on a paper towel and softly blot dry. Dip strawberries in chocolate and then lay them on wax paper to dry. Or dip strawberries using a toothpick and turn strawberries upside down and insert toothpick into a piece of Styrofoam to allow chocolate to dry.

#99

Chocolate-Covered Pretzels

MAKES 10–12 SERVINGS

1 bag (11.5 ounces)	**semisweet or milk chocolate chips**
2 tablespoons	**shortening or butter**
1 bag (10 ounces)	**pretzel rods**
3	**Butterfinger candy bars, crushed**
1 bag (8 ounces)	**toffee bits**

In a small slow cooker, melt chocolate chips with shortening or butter on high heat. Turn heat to low. Dip pretzels in chocolate and then roll in Butterfingers or toffee bits or both. Lay them on wax paper to dry.

Variation: Try rolling chocolate dipped pretzel in crushed candy canes for Christmas.

#100

Berry Chocolate Bars

MAKES 16 BARS

1 cup	**flour**
1/4 cup	**powdered sugar**
1/2 cup	**butter or margarine, softened**
1/2 cup	**strawberry, raspberry, or blueberry jam**
1 package (8 ounces)	**cream cheese, softened**
2 tablespoons	**milk**
1 cup	**white chocolate chips, melted**

Glaze:

3/4 cup	**semisweet chocolate chips**
1 tablespoon	**shortening or butter**

Preheat oven to 375 degrees.

Mix flour and powdered sugar together. Cut butter into flour mixture until crumbly. Press mixture into a 9 x 9-inch pan. Bake 15–18 minutes, or until lightly brown; cool completely. Spread jam over crust.

In a small bowl, mix cream cheese and milk together. Mix in melted white chocolate until smooth. Spread cream cheese mixture over jam. Refrigerate 1 hour.

For the glaze, melt chocolate chips and shortening or butter together. Spread chocolate over bars. Chill another hour, or until ready to serve.

#101

Cream Puff Squares

MAKES 24–28 SQUARES

1 cup	**water**
½ cup	**butter or margarine**
1 cup	**flour**
4	**eggs**
3 cups	**milk**
2 small boxes	**white chocolate instant pudding mix**
1 package (8 ounces)	**cream cheese, softened**
1 container (12 ounces)	**frozen whipped topping, thawed**
	chocolate syrup

Preheat oven to 400 degrees.

In a 2-quart pan, bring water and butter to a boil. Stir in flour until mixture forms a ball; remove from heat. Beat in eggs one at a time until smooth. Spread dough into a greased baking sheet. Bake 25–28 minutes, or until golden brown; cool completely.

In a 2-quart bowl, beat milk and pudding mixes together. Beat cream cheese into pudding mixture. Spread pudding mixture over cooled crust. Spread whipped topping over pudding. Drizzle chocolate syrup decoratively over the top.

NOTES

Metric Conversion Chart

VOLUME MEASUREMENTS		WEIGHT MEASUREMENTS		TEMPERATURE CONVERSION	
U.S.	Metric	U.S.	Metric	Fahrenheit	Celsius
1 teaspoon	5 ml	½ ounce	15 g	250	120
1 tablespoon	15 ml	1 ounce	30 g	300	150
¼ cup	60 ml	3 ounces	90 g	325	160
⅓ cup	75 ml	4 ounces	115 g	350	180
½ cup	125 ml	8 ounces	225 g	375	190
⅔ cup	150 ml	12 ounces	350 g	400	200
¾ cup	175 ml	1 pound	450 g	425	220
1 cup	250 ml	2¼ pounds	1 kg	450	230

About the Author

Stephanie Ashcraft was raised in Indiana. She received a bachelor's degree in family science and a teaching certificate from Brigham Young University. Stephanie loves teaching, interacting with people, and spending time with friends and family. She has taught hundreds of classes and appeared on hundreds of television and news programs all over the country sharing ways families can save time and money in the kitchen. Stephanie and her husband, Ivan, reside in Salem, Utah, with their children.